GREAT PIANO LITERATURE

focus on Melody

VOLUME 2

INTERMEDIATE/ EARLY ADVANCED

Selected and Edited by
SUZANNE GUY and
VICTORIA McARTHUR

Expressive and exciting masterworks with melodic exercises and performance suggestions

T0014689

THE
F·J·H
MUSIC
COMPANY
INC.
Frank J. Hackinson

Production: Frank and Gail Hackinson
Production Coordinator: Philip Groeber
Consulting Editor: Edwin McLean
Cover: Terpstra Design, San Francisco
Cover Photo: Ed Birch/Unicorn Stock Photos
Engraving: Tempo Music Press, Inc.
Printer: Tempo Music Press, Inc.

CONTENTS

"In Order of Appearance"

Note: Works are arranged by period and in approximate order of difficulty.

Contents by Composer

"Starring"

From the Authors...

MELODY TAKES CENTER STAGE

Before a melody can be heard, it must be born in the composer's mind. Then it is written down on paper, and eventually engraved as a finished composition. Finally, the performer must discover how to bring the melody to life and convey it to listeners so that they understand the composer's musical message. Many of the compositions in this volume were selected with Prokofiev's challenge in mind: "I must write a melody that, on the one hand is understandable to the average listener, and at the same time it must be original."

Singable tunes immediately captivate the listener, yet it takes practice to learn to make the piano "sing." One needs to look no further than the recordings of Vladimir Horowitz to find extraordinary models of melodic projection. It is said that Horowitz had the uncanny ability to place his ears in the twentieth row of every performance hall in which he played. His secret was to play the piano from the piano bench, yet hear from the audience seats.

This book can help students learn to recognize and interpret many different melodic settings in varied "starring roles." Through the playing of this compelling music, pianists will further learn to spotlight melodies, project their character, and share them with listeners.

WHAT MAKES A GREAT MELODY?

No one really knows what makes a great melody. Scientists can't measure it; composers can't follow a blueprint in order to duplicate it; performers and their listeners can't describe it using mere words. Yet there is a magical moment when a melody is clearly understood to be great.

It is hard to hum a melody that has touched you without also imagining its rhythm and harmony. Although melody is generally "the star" in most piano music, it must rely on its "supporting cast and other players" (i.e., rhythm, harmony) to project the music's complete story. It is fascinating to observe that we can recognize many melodies alone (without rhythm or harmony) after several exposures to the complete musical setting. The mind fills in the missing elements–the complete and vivid musical snapshot which has been imprinted on our memory from prior experiences with the music. This is a demonstration of the powerful effect of melody on human consciousness.

SHINING THE SPOTLIGHT ON MELODY

WHERE TO FIND THE MELODY

Typically there are three possible locations for the melody:

1. In the upper (top or soprano) voice
2. In the lower (bottom or bass) voice
3. In an inner voice

Usually the melody can be found in an upper voice, with lower voice melodies
next most frequent in occurrence.

Sonata in E Major

Domenico Scarlatti

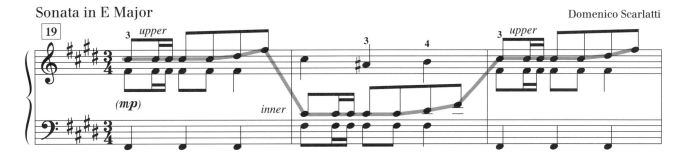

Always look carefully at note stems. Composers often give clues to melodic location
through the melody notes' stem directions in relation to the surrounding notes. Look
especially closely at notes with extra note stems ("double-stemmed").

Sonata in C♯ Minor

Ludwig van Beethoven

Longer rhythmic values or specially articulated notes (tenutos, accents, etc.) may also indicate a
melody line.

Doctor Gradus ad Parnassum

Claude Debussy

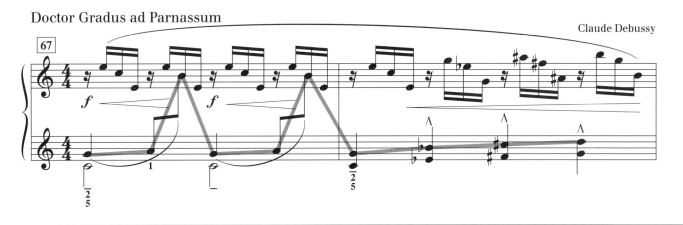

How to Follow the Melody

The pianist is similar to the stage crew member who operates the spotlight. The spotlighter must know which actors (melody notes) to follow. The spotlight must follow smoothly, constantly widening or tightening, intensifying or muting, coloring, focusing or unfocusing—always helping the audience follow the action on stage.

Tip: Consider highlighting melodies with different color marking pens. Make the primary melody yellow, the secondary melodies (if any), another color.

Visions Fugitives — Sergei Prokofiev

How Do You Shape a Melody?

Sing it! It is the easiest and most effective way to define the melodic contour and determine the natural places to let the music breathe.

Arietta — Edvard Grieg

Tip: *Play only the melody first. Use the indicated fingering (or play each note with fingers 3 and 1 pressed together).*
Add pedal to color and shape the main melody. Listen for expressive tone.

...First Comes the Ear

The melodic shape must first be fixed in the ear, then projected through the fingers.
Help conceptualize the melody more clearly with any of these suggestions:

- sing (or whistle or vocalize with syllables or words)
- dance, move, or conduct
- assign characters and act them out
- write lyrics or develop a story
- mentally "orchestrate" with instruments other than piano
- listen to good recordings

...Then Come the Fingers

Listen to the rise and fall of the melody as you play, with the ear guiding you from one
note to the next. Melodies are either going toward or moving away from some musical
landmark. Use dynamic contrasts (e.g., *cresc.* and *dim.*) to musically highlight this point.

Mazurka in G Minor   Frédéric Chopin

A legato melody should sound more like a smooth velvet cord than like knots on a rough
rope. Match the end of one tone to the beginning of the next one. Listen carefully to short
note values that follow long note values to avoid unmusical accents.

Sonata in C♯ Minor   Ludwig van Beethoven

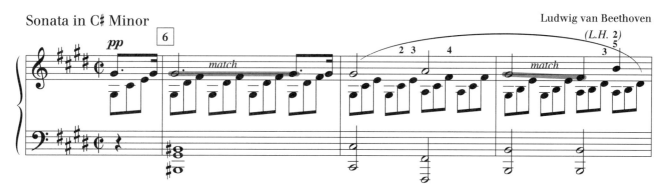

A change in register (a melodic leap to another octave) is an opportunity for a change
in tone color. Experiment with sounds that match an orchestral instrument. This is one
of the piano's greatest attributes—to sound like instruments other than itself.

Sonata in C Minor   Giovanni Battista Pescetti

MELODIC EXERCISES: Getting Ready for the Spotlight

MELODIC TONE

"Speak with an expressive voice"

Melodic Tone Exercise No. 1

Play these variations on Hanon's *Preparatory Exercise No. 1* with both hands
two octaves apart (right hand one octave higher than written in the original).

Variations:

1. Play in the original key of C, then transpose to C♯, then D.

2. Use different articulations, such as R.H. *staccato*, L.H. *legato*. Then
   reverse the articulations (R.H. *legato*, L.H. *staccato*).

3. Use different dynamics than written, such as R.H. *forte*, L.H. *piano*. Then reverse
   dynamics for the hands. For sensitive dynamic inflection, listen intently so you
   never play more than three notes in a row at *exactly* the same dynamic level.

Exercise No. 1 (revised)

C.L. Hanon

Melodic Tone Exercise No. 2

Many pianists would agree that a singing tone has the following characteristics:

1. resonance (the sound continues to ring)

2. richness (intensity), so the sound projects and carries far beyond the dimensions
   of the piano

3. absence of non-musical noise, such as the percussive sound of the finger striking the key,
   clicking of fingernails, or the sound of the key mechanism at either the top or
   bottom of the key movement

Listen for the above three characteristics as you play the Chopin *Prelude* chords below.

Chords from *Prelude* Op. 28, No. 9

Frédéric Chopin

*May be omitted for small hands.

BALANCE BETWEEN HANDS

"Stars, co-stars, supporting cast"

Balance Ear-Training Exercise

Notice how your ear is drawn to the higher sounds in music.

To help train your ear to listen for the melody when it is not high, play any piece (especially from the Baroque or Classical period) with the hands crossed (R.H. plays R.H. notes; L.H. plays L.H. notes–cross the R.H. over the L.H.). Both hands may be displaced one or more octaves to avoid crowding.

VOICING

"The star's voice could be heard over the crowd"

"Voicing" is the art of projecting the melody over competing voices within the same hand.

Voicing Exercise No. 1

Play these celebrated "Canon Chords" while changing pedal on every chord.

1. Voice (bring out) the bass line (L.H. octaves). Play it *forte*, at least two dynamic levels above the other voices.

2. Next, voice the soprano the same way.

3. Voice the alto.

4. Finally, voice the tenor.

Imagine you are playing on a nine-foot concert grand piano in a centuries-old cathedral with a high vaulted ceiling. Let every chord ring!

*optional

Voicing Exercise No. 2

Experiment with voicing in this Grieg *Lyric Piece*:

1. L.H. plays only lower (bass voice) quarter notes.

2. R.H. plays the up-stemmed melody notes *non legato* by using
   fingers 3 and 1 pressed together. Lift gently from the wrist
   and drop onto each melody note as you play.

3. Play only the sixteenth notes, divided between the two hands. The flowing stream
   of sixteenth notes must always sound as though they are being played by one
   hand. This is achieved with a gentle, undulating motion of the wrist.

4. Combine all three voices, using the indicated fingering. Listen intently, as though
   you were following a choir singing its parts.

5. Add pedal, changing every beat. Listen for a singing tone.

Arietta

Edvard Grieg

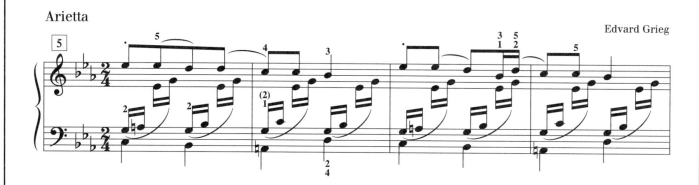

MELODIC DIRECTION

"A star improves with good direction"

Melodic Direction Exercise

1. Each of the 16 eighth notes in this melody leads to the dotted-quarter note G
   in measure 37.

2. "Pull" each note from the arm as the finger slides toward you on the key. Keep
   the arm and wrist supple.

3. Listen for a subtle color and dynamic change on each repeated D as it responds
   to the changing harmonies underneath.

4. Strive to create the effect of forward motion when progressing from one
   melody note to the next.

Fantasia in D Minor

Wolfgang A. Mozart

BAROQUE
(1600–1750)

"Remember that much of J.S. Bach is not idiomatic keyboard music, but an imitation of voices, instruments, or ensembles, and uses the resources of the piano accordingly."
—Ralph Kirkpatrick, harpsichordist

MELODIC FEATURES:

- Generally one of two different characters is expressed: either melodies that "dance," or melodies that "sing."
- There are few dynamic extremes—melodies are generally neither too soft nor too loud, reflecting the capabilities of the keyboard at the time.
- Counterpoint—melody set against another (or the same) melody—is a common feature.
- Melodies are often ornamented to add further melodic, rhythmic, or coloristic effects.

EDITORIAL MARKINGS

The editors have added:

- Dynamics (indicated in parentheses) and articulations which are based on the performance conventions of the time, and include considerations for the distinctive qualities of the modern piano.
- Tempo and metronome markings, and character markings (indicated in parentheses), based on the appropriate style of the music.
- Fingerings that fit the average hand and, in the authors' opinions, come closest to assuring successful performance.
- Historically appropriate ornaments have been added and/or realized (see *ossias* above the staff) which may be modified or sometimes deleted entirely depending on personal taste or technical ease.

AUTHENTICITY

The editors have consulted autographs and/or first editions, when available. Regardless, for most works, at least three other reputable editions were studied in order to assure the accuracy of the score.

This particular gavotte is as melodic as it is rhythmic, since all three voices are tuneful. Be sure to notice the stemming of the upper voices, showing clearly the soprano and alto lines. It is traditional to favor the higher voice, but the repeats offer an opportunity to bring out the running bass line in measures 4–7. In the second half, spotlight the lower voice (measures 12–15) for contrast on the repeat.

Gavotte

(from *French Suite No. 5 in G Major*)

JOHANN SEBASTIAN BACH
(1685–1750)

(Allegretto) (♩ = 72-80)

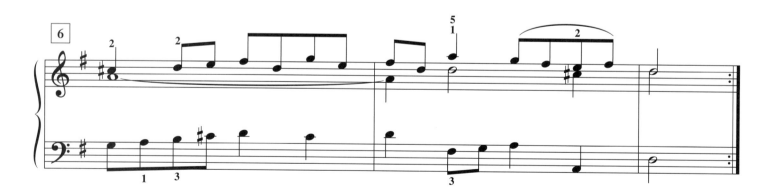

Note: ♩ = non legato; ♪♪ and ♩ = legato

The title means "a repeating bass line from G to C." Each group of eight measures repeats a harmonic progression, with the melody varied above it. The right hand is constantly expanding or contracting to accommodate all the changing melodic intervals. Measures 13–15 are interesting due to the succession of leaps in the right hand. These are more effective melodically if you emphasize the lower as well as the upper note of each interval.

A Ground in Gamut

Z. 645

HENRY PURCELL
(1659–1695)

*Purcell originally notated this as

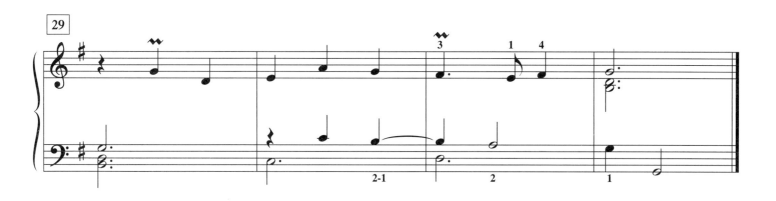

Following the melodic line for each of the four voices challenges the ear. Notice that one voice always moves forward–the bass at measure 2; the tenor at measure 4; the bass and soprano in duet at measure 6. The lilting rhythm has a calming effect. In fact, its predictability allows for a quasi-improvisatory approach to playing the melodies and ornaments. This is an excellent piece to become comfortable with two baroque ornaments, mordents (✹ ♫♩) and four-note trills (✹ ♫♫♩).

Siciliana

(from *Suite in D Minor*)

Gottlieb Muffat
(1690–1770)

It is easy to play this sonata as a technical display piece; it is much more challenging and rewarding to project its continuous melodic quality. Every note of each triplet figure demands attentive listening. Do not shorten the left-hand quarter notes too much, since they are the underpinning of the melody. Notice additional voicing possibilities (in measures 9–27 and all similar places) for left-hand countermelodies.

Sonata No. 6 in C Minor

3rd movement

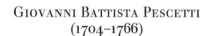

Giovanni Battista Pescetti
(1704–1766)

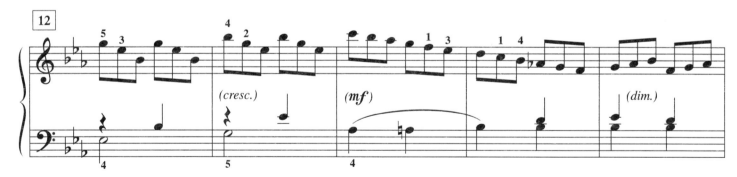

This lovely transcription by Bach of the *Adagio* from Marcello's oboe concerto is clearly reminiscent of the oboe's penetrating voice. The first three measures set the stage for a soaring melody. The repeated chords and intervals played by the left hand offer rhythmic stability which allows the single-line melody to unwind at will. It may be helpful to listen to a recording of the original oboe concerto as Marcello wrote it.

Concerto in D Minor

BWV 974, 2nd movement

JOHANN SEBASTIAN BACH (1685–1750)
TRANSCRIBED FOR KEYBOARD FROM *OBOE CONCERTO IN D MINOR*, ALESSANDRO MARCELLO

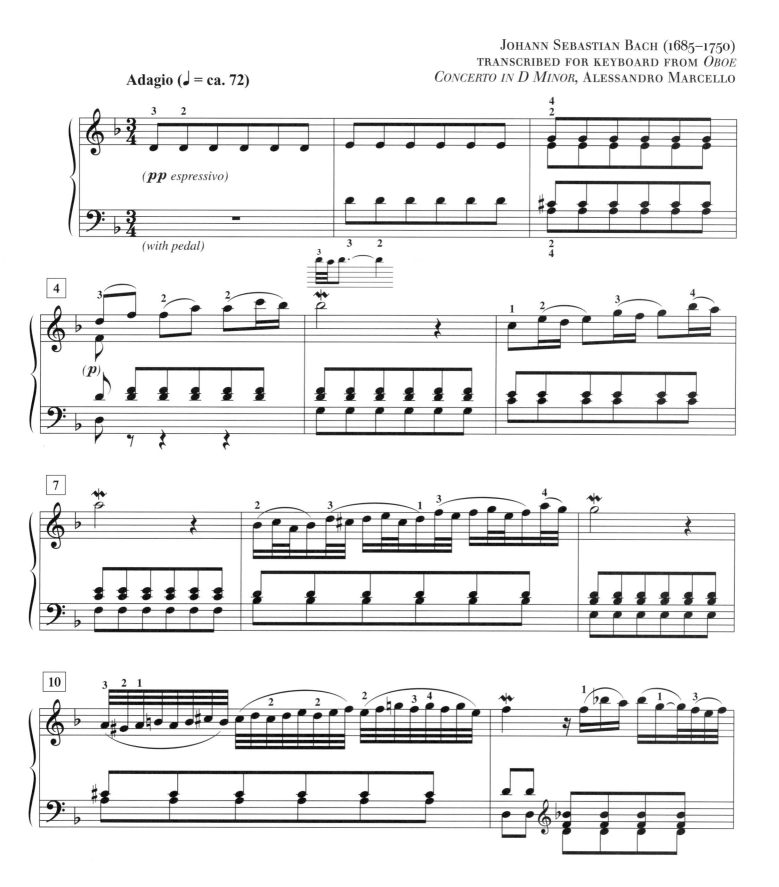

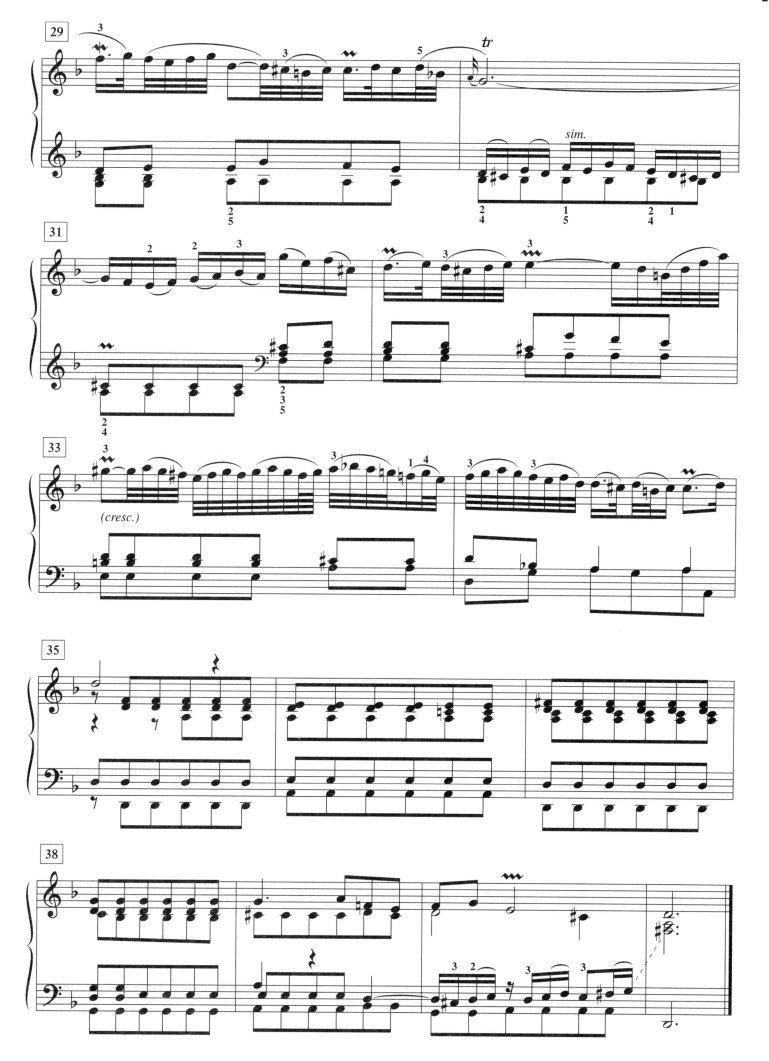

Vladimir Horowitz began many of his recitals with Scarlatti sonatas. This was one of his favorites, and it may likely be one of yours. Horowitz's name is synonymous with tonal color and imaginative "orchestration," just the pianistic prescription needed in this piece. Notice three especially important features: the dotted rhythm typical of a polonaise (measure 1), the open fifths (measure 2, measures 19–21), and a series of repeated two-note slurs (measure 22 and all similar places). Think of the open fifths as trumpet or horn calls, bold and triumphant. Use your imagination to create these and other special effects.

Sonata in E Major
K. 380, L. 23

DOMENICO SCARLATTI
(1685–1757)

CLASSICAL
(1750–1820)

"No one pays to hear an Alberti bass (accompaniment). You come to a concert to hear the melody."
—Jorge Bolet, pianist

MELODIC FEATURES:

- A single-line melody is most common, often accompanied by a transparent harmonic accompaniment.

- Scales or broken chords often form the basis for melody.

- Melodies usually appear in four- or eight-measure phrases or other regular phrase lengths.

- The idea of melodic "themes" becomes important as more extended musical forms develop (sonata form, theme and variations, etc.).

- While the Baroque period often highlights more than one melody at the same time (counterpoint), in the Classical period, melodies are presented one after the other.

- Ornaments lose much of their improvisatory character, yet still serve an important melodic purpose.

- Dynamics become an important part of expression, taking advantage of the developing pianoforte.

EDITORIAL MARKINGS

The editors have added:

- A few dynamics and marks of articulation.

- Some tempo and character markings. All metronome markings are editorial.

- Fingerings.

- Historically appropriate ornaments have been suggested and/or realized (see *ossias* above the staff).

AUTHENTICITY

The editors have consulted autographs and/or first editions, when available. Regardless, for most works, at least three other reputable editions were studied in order to assure the accuracy of the score.

very sixteenth note in this piece is melodic, but not every note should have the same melodic inflection. Follow the dynamic markings, and the contrasts will be dramatic and exciting. This short yet effective showpiece is made up of patterns of scale fragments and broken chords.

Fantasia in G Major

Wq. 117:8

CARL PHILIPP EMANUEL BACH
(1714–1788)

Note: ♩ and ♪ = non legato; ♪ = legato

There is an almost folk-like quality to both themes of the exposition (measures 1–30). Even after one hearing, the tunes stay in the head. Note the *sf* markings that appear in measures 5–7 (and similarly throughout the movement) should be emphasized but never forced. The development (measures 31–50) is particularly dramatic, with an abrupt shift to minor, along with the only left-hand melodic content in the movement. Sail through those scales for an exciting ending!

Sonatina in C Major

Op. 151, No. 4, 1st movement

ANTON DIABELLI
(1781–1858)

Allegro moderato (♩ = ca. 132)

Although, at first glance, this movement appears to be one continuous melodic sweep, there is surprising structure in this *sonata quasi una fantasia*. The primary theme (measures 5–15) and the secondary theme (measures 15–23) are almost seamless in melodic tone quality. But it is the more active bass line in the secondary theme which creates the contrasting impact. The melody and harmony intertwine to form one of the most exquisitely beautiful pieces ever written.

Sonata in C# Minor

Op. 27, No. 2, 1st movement

LUDWIG VAN BEETHOVEN
(1770–1827)

*This entire movement should be played very delicately and with pedal.

FJH1226

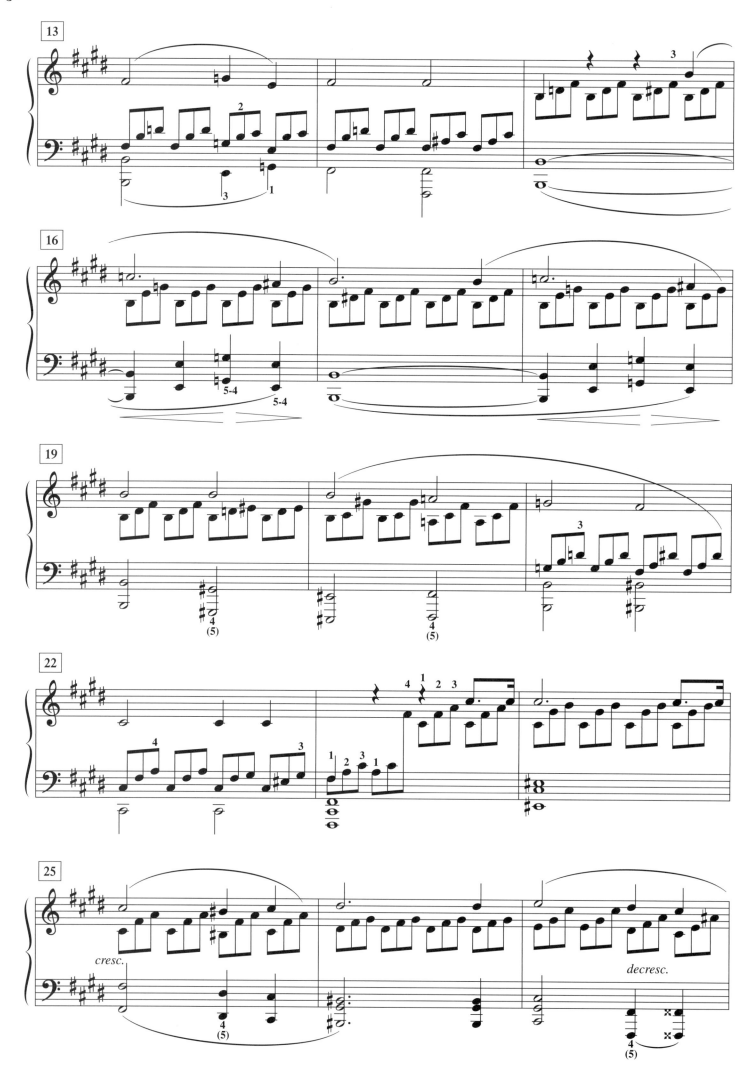

It will help your understanding of this piece to look over the score first; then play it slowly and listen. In the opening theme, the melody centers around the dominant (the fifth note) of the key. In the next eight-measure phrase, this dominant note (C) is repeated 14 times in a row. Take care! So much repetition can sound as though you're tuning the piano! Instead, shape the repeated notes into expressive statements. Each time the A theme returns (measures 34–49 and measures 58–65), its melody is slightly varied, gaining in charm and ingenuity each time.

Bagatelle in F Major

Op. 33, No. 3

LUDWIG VAN BEETHOVEN
(1770–1827)

42

FJH1226

Mozart's operatic voice speaks throughout this fantasy. Emphasize depth of tone by playing deeply into the keys in the opening *Andante*. Every note in the long phrases is melodic, each one melting into the next to create a seamless veil of sound. As the *Adagio* arrives, imagine the soprano waiting offstage to make her entrance, then singing her emotional aria. The charming melody that begins the *Allegretto* (at measure 55) marks the arrival of happier times. Mozart's expressive use of silence is very powerful throughout this piece. Be sure to observe the full value of all the rests in order to act out this drama.

Fantasia in D Minor

K. 397

WOLFGANG AMADEUS MOZART
(1756–1791)

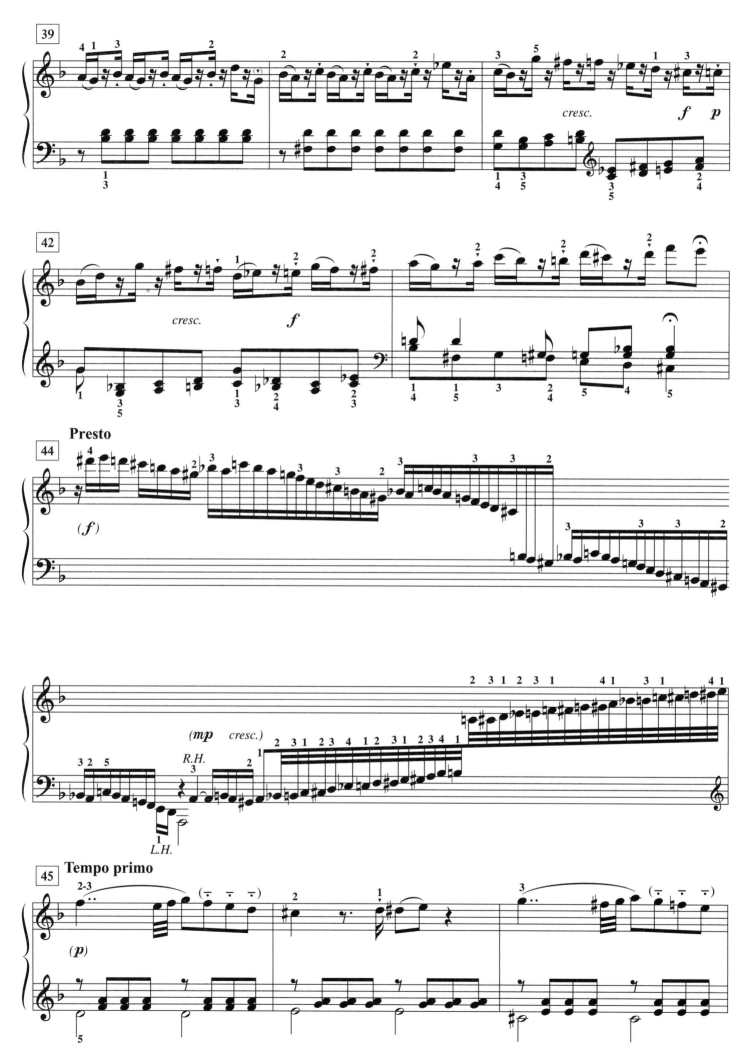

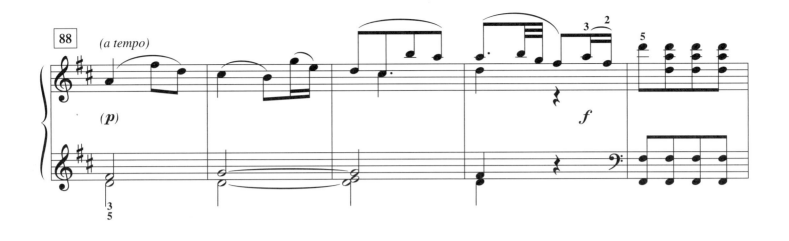

ROMANTIC

(1820–1900)

"Fair Melody! Kind Siren! I've no choice;
I must be thy sad servant evermore;
I cannot choose but kneel here and adore."
—John Keats, poet

MELODIC FEATURES:

Melodies:

- Come to the forefront as the most prominent feature.
- Become longer and more complex, developing in tandem with generally lengthening musical forms.
- Express a vivid spectrum of emotions, shedding what were thought to be the mannered inhibitions of the past.
- Become more dramatic as well as more intimate, and often served to "show off" the skills of the famous performers.
- Explore the expanded registers of the larger and more powerful piano.
- Countermelodies appear in increasingly thicker and more complex musical textures.

EDITORIAL MARKINGS

The editors have added:

- Some fingerings and marks of articulation.
- Dynamics, which in a few cases, have been further clarified.
- Tempo, metronome, or character markings, which appear in parentheses.
- Suggested pedaling.

Chopin's shortest piece, only 13 measures, emphasizes sheer sonority. Although every measure has the same rhythmic motive, it is fascinating to experiment with different voicing. Measures 5–8 and measures 9–12 can sound "light" or "dark," depending on whether the upper or middle voice leads. The fifth fingers of both hands should feel like steel in order to support full arm weight on each chord. Be sure to notice the contrast of the left-hand chromaticism in measures 5–6, and how different the effect is from the larger left-hand leaps in the opening.

Prelude in C Minor

Op. 28, No. 20

FRÉDÉRIC CHOPIN
(1810–1849)

Chopin wrote these Polish nationalistic dances throughout his life. In this mazurka there are three interesting melodies, each one starring the right hand. The principal melody has a longing quality, made more poignant because it was one of the last that Chopin wrote. An energetic grace note introduces the second theme at measure 17. The unaccompanied eight-measure theme (starting at measure 33) should have an expressive legato. ("Cover" the hammer sound by overlapping the legato connection between tones.) Let the piece unwind back to the first melody.

Mazurka in G Minor

Op. 67, No. 2

FRÉDÉRIC CHOPIN
(1810–1849)

*This is Chopin's original tempo. The editors suggest ♩ = ca. 126.

54

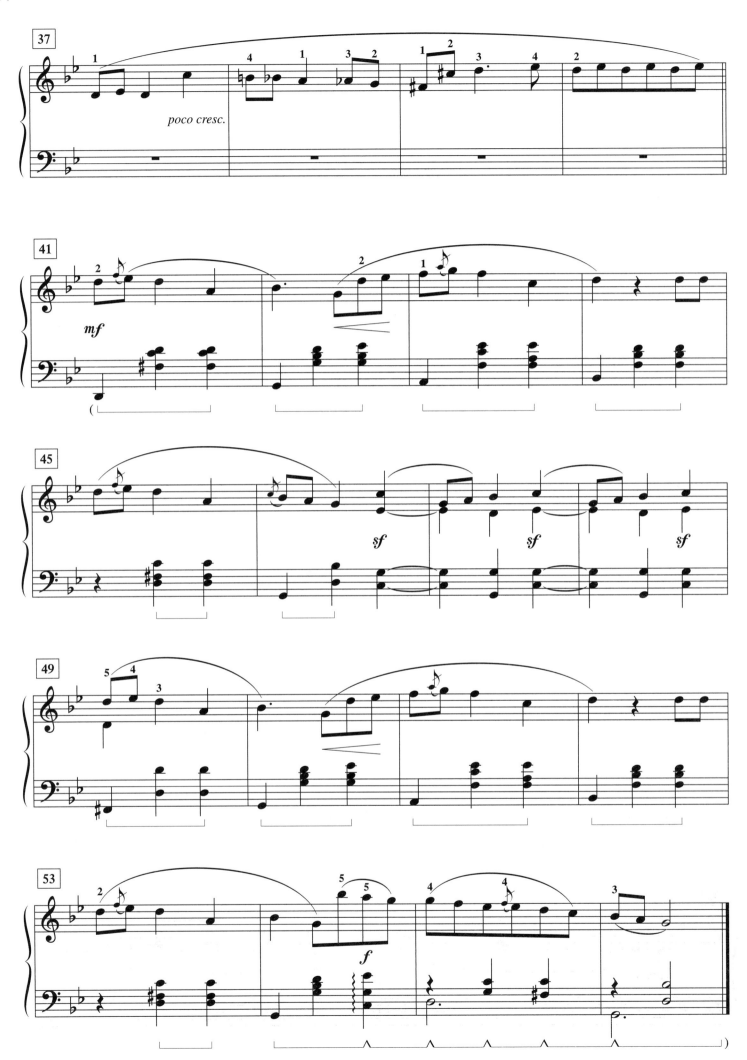

Be sure to feel this waltz in two-measure groups of six beats for a continuous flow of melody. Emphasize every other downbeat as you mimic breathing. "Inhale" the first measure and "exhale" the second. There should be a certain richness and warmth in the sound at the key change to B major (measure 9). Listen carefully to the melody in measures 14 and 15, where the right-hand thumb carries the alto line. Notice the few melodic moments for the bass (measures 8 and 9) to sing out.

Waltz in G♯ Minor

Op. 39, No. 3

JOHANNES BRAHMS
(1833–1897)

This lovely melody fits neatly in four-measure groups which predictably rise and fall melodically. Think of inhaling as the melody rises, and exhaling as the melody falls. At measure 17, the composer marked "pleadingly," advice left to the performer's imagination for this duet between the prince and princess. The return of the first theme at measure 33 should sound more longing than at the beginning. Experiment with *una corda* pedal effects on the second page to highlight the dreamy, romantic mood.

Sung Outside the Prince's Door

(from *Forgotten Fairy Tales*, Op. 4, No. 1)

EDWARD MacDOWELL
(1860–1908)

*Many editions transpose this piece to the key of G major. The original key of G♭ major is darker and more beautiful.

The left-hand repeated chords should be "brushed" by pressing gently with a firm touch. Maintain control and avoid any percussiveness by staying close to the key surface. Beginning at measures 5–8 in the bass clef, separate note stems indicate melodic interest in the tenor line which parallels the soprano melody at the interval of a tenth. Note the composer's accents for the most important melody notes, which must be emphasized but not punched. The lovely five-measure coda recalls the opening theme, now played with the left hand (crossing over the R.H. chords) that fade away.

Etude in E Major

Op. 47, No. 16

Stephen Heller
(1813–1888)

This is one of the shortest and most beautiful of Grieg's 66 *Lyric Pieces*. Notice an unusual feature in this piece—the first and last measures contain identical notes, while other markings such as dynamics vary. Be sure to project these important details in your interpretation. Each of the three voices has been assigned its own rhythm pattern, with the soprano line always managing to stay in the spotlight. The middle voice is divided between the strong first and second fingers of both hands. Take care to create a quiet but rhythmic harp-like sound here.

Arietta

(from *Lyric Pieces,* Op. 12, No. 1)

EDVARD GRIEG
(1843–1907)

Poco andante e sostenuto (♪ = ca. 84-100)

*Grieg's original pedal markings are indicated. The editors suggest harmonic pedaling throughout.

Visual images associated with water are helpful in this *Venetian Boat Song*, especially for the left hand. Use a sinking gesture on the first and fourth eighth notes of each measure as the arm glides to navigate the large intervals. There is a clear harmonic and melodic climax at measure 30, where the C♯ major dominant has never seemed more dramatic. Note the long pedal marking that creates a harmonic backdrop for the melody.

Venetian Boat Song

Op. 30, No. 6

FELIX MENDELSSOHN
(1809–1847)

This is the most famous theme from Rachmaninoff's beloved second piano concerto, in a version for solo piano written by the composer himself. Each statement of the theme is more intense than the one before. The second thematic statement at measure 17 is especially rich, with octaves in the right hand and streaming arpeggios in the left hand. Rachmaninoff was a wonderful pianist who balanced a successful concert career with his composing. He pushed the resources of the piano, and of pianists also, in this well-beloved work. Pianists must have pillar-like fifth fingers for melody voicing, as well as the ability to release the weight of the entire upper body onto the keyboard for passages where the piano must sing out over the large orchestra.

(Theme from)
Concerto No. 2 in C Minor
Op. 18

COMPOSED AND TRANSCRIBED BY
SERGEI RACHMANINOFF
(1873–1943)

It is no coincidence that we think of Schumann when hearing this romance. His signature dotted rhythmic figure (♪♪) and contrapuntal texture is readily apparent. It takes an attentive ear to listen for a continuous singing line through the alto and soprano dialogue (measures 1–6). Notice how fresh and unusual the phrasing is, beginning with three-measure groups, followed by a long eight-measure response. The bass and tenor voices share a relaxed syncopation throughout.

Romance

Op. 15, No. 2

NIKOLAY RIMSKY-KORSAKOV
(1844–1908)

Andantino espressivo (♪ = ca. 120)

Even at first hearing, your ear will be drawn to this simple melody as it passes through several key changes and surprising harmonic excursions (Wagner's trademark). The unity of this composition comes from several repetitions of a 16-measure melody; the variety is in the treatment of both melody and accompaniment. The soprano sings the first statement in mostly two-voice texture, shadowed by the alto solo beautifully cradled between the soprano and bass (measures 17–21). Notice the tenor entrance at measure 27 on the third beat (it is easy to miss). Both hands share the melody beginning at measure 36. Amazingly, there is no real sense of tonal arrival until measure 66 when the key of C major feels settled. Pace the lengthy *rallentando* (measures 67 until the end) carefully in order to sustain interest.

Album Leaf in C Major

(1861)

RICHARD WAGNER
(1813–1883)

*Wagner's pedaling is shown in measures 42–44 and 63–68.

TWENTIETH CENTURY (CONTEMPORARY)
(1900–1999)

"The beauty and meaning of a melody depends on the mutual relations of the successive tones. Obliterate the memory of every note as soon as the next note is played, and there can be no melody."
—Albert Gehring, musicologist

MELODIC FEATURES:

The most striking feature is the huge range of styles.

Melodies show characteristics such as:

- Shifting of focus away from expressive melody, toward emphasis on harmony, rhythm, tone color, and texture.

- More disjunct (larger interval) melodic shape, as the emphasis shifts from the "singable" melody of the Romantic period.

- Common usage of scales other than major or minor (e.g., pentatonic, whole-tone, modes, etc.).

- Few distinctive or even discernable melodies in some styles.

- Borrowing of melodic styles from past historical periods (e.g., neo-classical, neo-romantic, etc.).

- Melody tones are dissonant with harmonic accompaniment in many cases.

EDITORIAL MARKINGS

Since most important 20th-century composers have lived to see the publication and widespread distribution and performance of their work, authentic and reliable performance markings are more generally the norm in most sources. Nonetheless, the editors have added fingering and pedaling, when needed. In rare cases, other marks have been added, and have been indicated as such in the score.

NOTE

Due to recent international copyright restrictions, few works are included with publication dates after 1923.

Four exquisitely melodic phrases make up this eighteen-measure Romanian Dance. Bartók also scored these dances for violin and piano. Thus, the left hand imitates a good pianist, and the right hand a fine violinist. Each pair of phrases has identical melodies, but the harmonies change. At measure 11, the melody grows in intensity until it is repeated gently, as if in a trance.

Buciumeana

(from *Romanian Dances*, No. 4)

BÉLA BARTÓK
(1881–1945)

Picture a solitary flutist playing as he soothes his sheep to sleep. Compare the different dynamic markings in each flute call (measures 1–4, measures 12–13, and measures 19–20). Articulate the jazzy rhythms in the little dances that follow the solos. Debussy gives precise directions for phrasing, dynamics, and countermelody articulation. Such attention to detail may have prompted Guy Maier's remark, "No human voice can produce the shimmering, sparkling, melodic line which Debussy exacts from the pianist's hands and feet."

The Little Shepherd
(from *Children's Corner*)

CLAUDE DEBUSSY
(1862–1918)

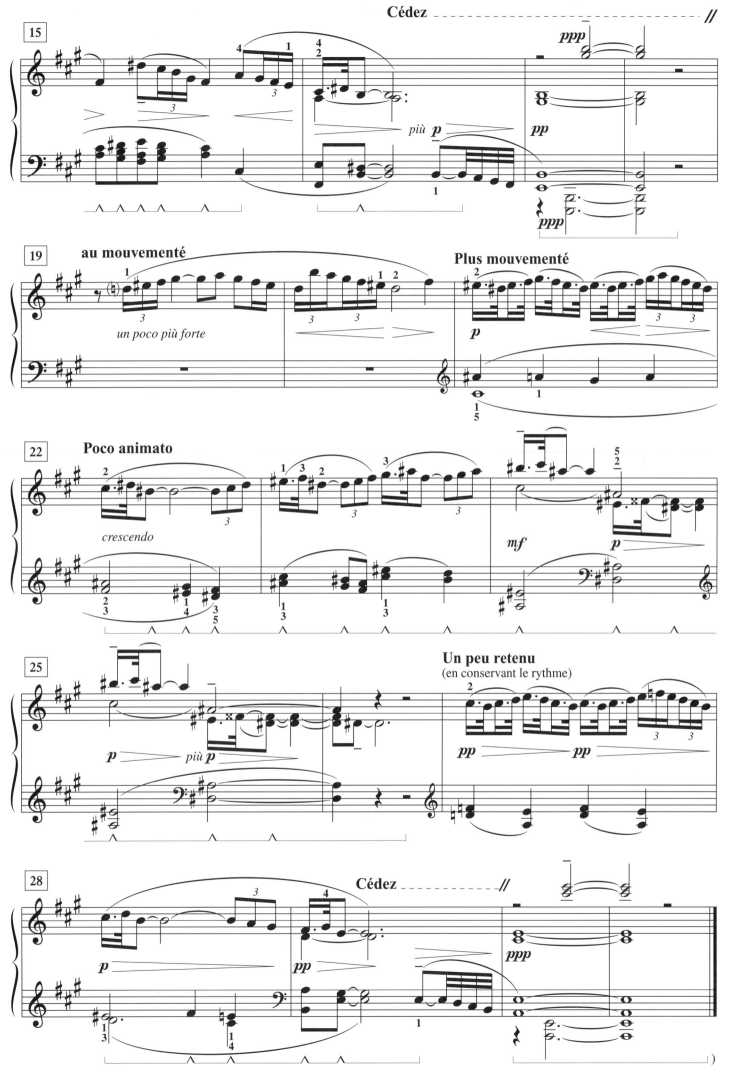

Kodály's primary instrument (although he also played piano and violin) was the cello. In this piece, the cello's melodic range is fully explored. The left-hand melody, reflecting a confluence of Hungarian folk song and French impressionism, has a sad, almost haunting quality. Study the score before playing and make mental notes of the many subtle tempo fluctuations, allowing for expressive "give" and "take."

Piano Piece

Op. 11, No. 7

ZOLTÁN KODÁLY
(1882–1967)

Lean toward the right for better body balance, since this piece begins quite high on the keyboard. The groups of three eighth notes, both in the accompaniment and the melody, should be played with small wrist circles, as if rolling from note to note. Aim for a climax in measure 19, and a rich sound at measure 31 in the left hand. The challenge lies in the ability to project the melody even though the dynamic level is rarely above *mezzo piano*. This piece deserves to be better known, as it is exquisitely beautiful.

Dream

(from *Enfantines*)

ERNEST BLOCH
(1880–1959)

The first piece in the *Children's Corner* is a delightful spoof on Clementi's famous set of exercises, *Gradus ad Parnassum*. Picture a typical piano student who is bored with repetitive exercises. Three times the frustrated practicer begins with good intentions, but soon wanders off to more interesting sounds and experimental harmonies. Upon arrival at the coda, the pianist is on a runaway roller coaster that stops abruptly at the bottom of the keyboard. Never let the melody get lost among all the sixteenth notes!

Doctor Gradus ad Parnassum

(from *Children's Corner*)

CLAUDE DEBUSSY
(1862–1918)

Note: *m.g. (main gauche)* = left hand
     m.d. (main droit) = right hand

*optional fingering

FJH1226

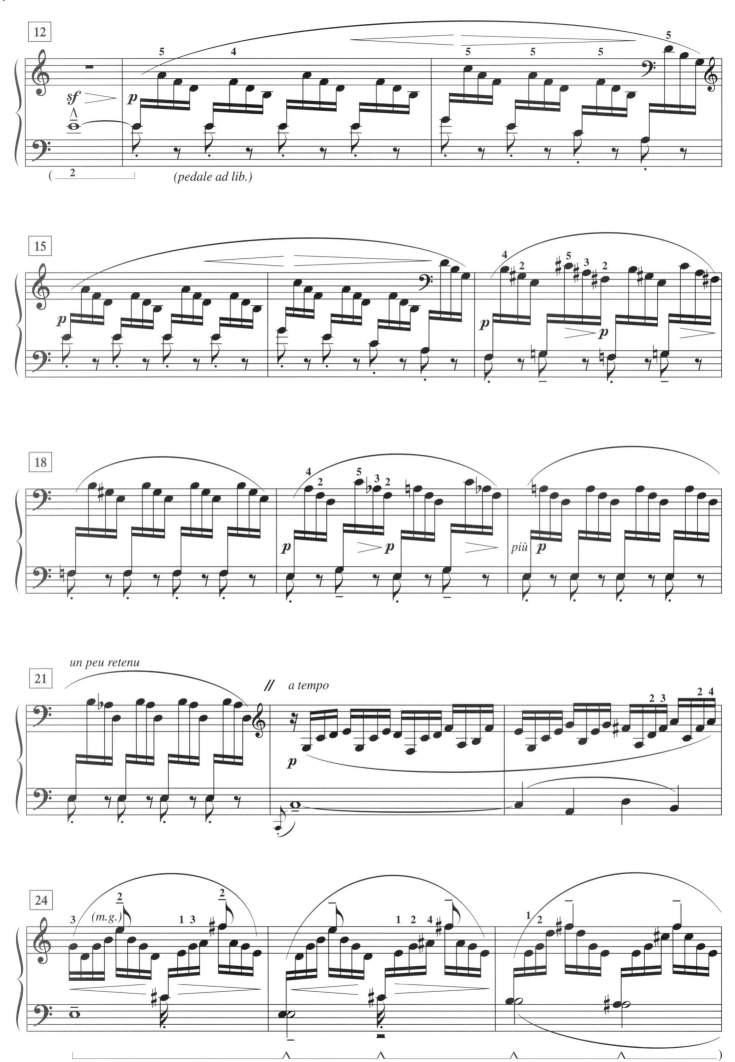

Make sure your eyes and ears are ready before you approach this fascinating piece. Everywhere you look there is a melody! The three-voice texture continues until measure 19, when four voices interweave until the end. The ear should listen for the chromatic soprano line, but notice the alto joining in its own chromaticism. A series of two-note slurs enters at measure 9 and intensifies as countermelodies join the cast.

Visions Fugitives

Op. 22, No. 16

Sergei Prokofiev
(1891–1953)

As you play this beautiful melody, release more weight into the lowest notes in the accompanying bass line for greater depth of sound. Think of every four-measure phrase as a little wave. Breathe in for four measures, breathe out for four more–this pattern repeats throughout the piece. The waves begin to build at measure 25 and peak at measure 33. Be sure to arrive at the *sf* marking on the high G, supported by the low E♭ (the first time the melody has been accompanied on the downbeat). Granados created a special ending–heavenly bells that fade softly in the distance.

Epílogo

(from *Escenas Románticas,* No. 6)

ENRIQUE GRANADOS
(1867–1916)

Andantino spianato (♩ = ca. 108)

con exaltación poética

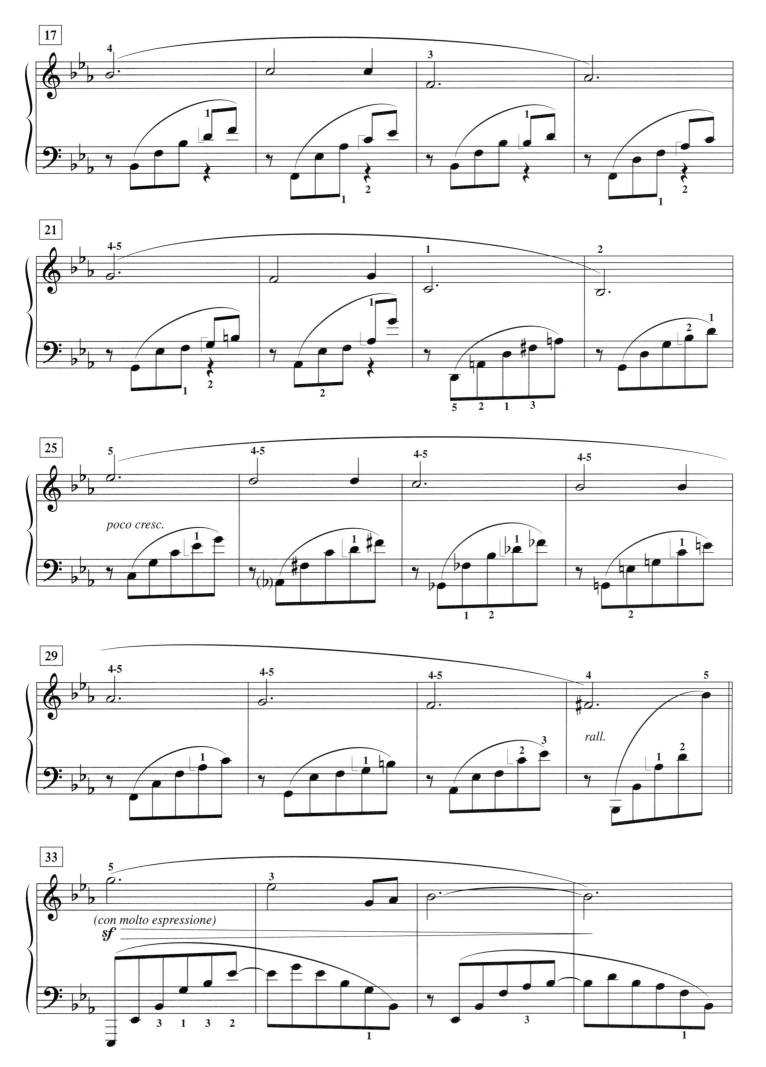

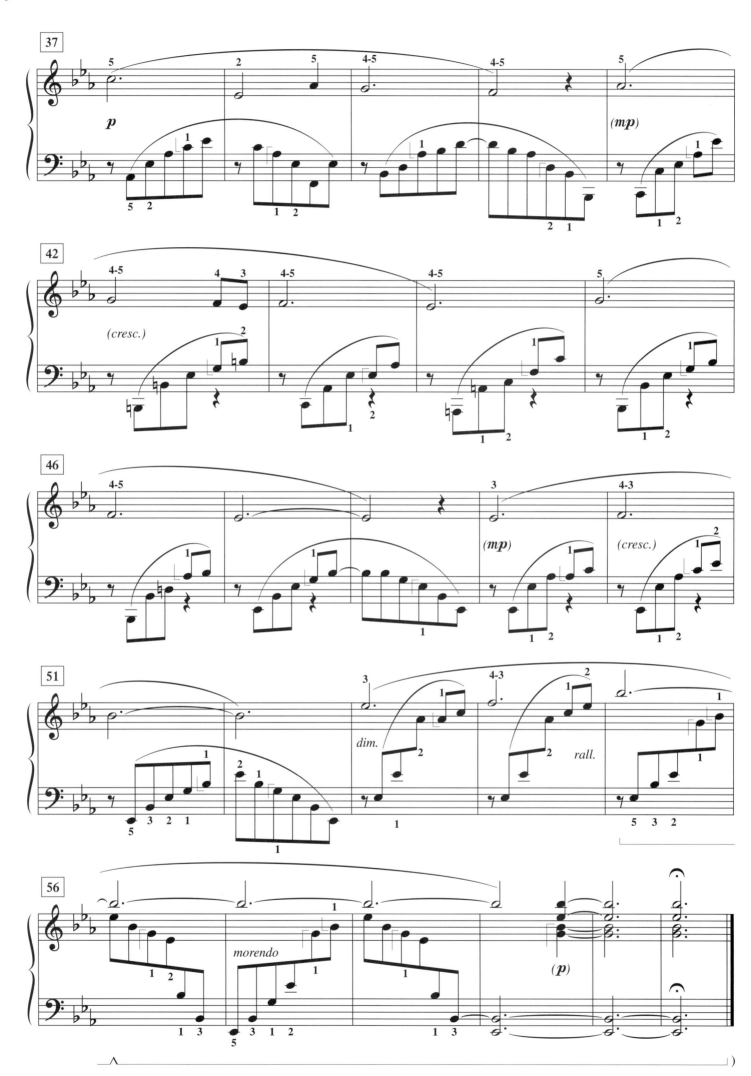

Biographical Information for Composers

Bach, Carl Philipp Emanuel (C.P.E.) (1714–1788, Germany)
C.P.E. was the second oldest son of J.S. Bach, and is generally considered the finest composer among Bach's children. His *Essay on the True Art of Keyboard Playing* is still consulted as a reference for the correct performance of baroque music. His works are highly expressive and dramatic.

Bach, Johann Sebastian (1685–1750, Germany)
Bach's dates define the High Baroque Period. He spent his life as a composer, organist, choirmaster, and father of and musical influence on his 23 children. Bach was well known primarily as a performer during his lifetime. His brilliant work was brought to the world's attention by Felix Mendelssohn almost 100 years after Bach's death. Bach's compositions are catalogued as BWV (Bach-Werke-Verzeichnis/Bach-Works-Catalog).

Bartók, Béla (1881–1945, Hungary)
Bartók was a musicologist as well as a composer, and traveled across his native Hungary recording over 6000 folk songs. His music is rich with folk melodies and dances. Bartók also had a great interest in writing music for young people.

Beethoven, Ludwig van (1770–1827, Germany)
Arguably the most recognized name in classical music, Beethoven wrote many of the world's favorite classical themes: *Ode to Joy, Für Elise, Moonlight Sonata,* the *Fifth Symphony,* as well as others. Beethoven's early works are in the classical style, while his later works are decidedly romantic in content. He began to grow deaf in adulthood and wrote his last masterpieces with only his inner hearing to guide him.

Bloch, Ernest (1880–1959, Switzerland/U.S.)
Bloch's compositional style borrows both from romanticism and impressionism. He became a U.S. citizen in 1924 and taught at the Mannes School in New York.

Brahms, Johannes (1833–1897, Germany)
Brahms was generally deemed to be the heir-apparent to Beethoven. Most of Brahms' piano works are quite difficult, demanding large hands and a strong singing tone. His works for piano include short character pieces as well as lengthy sonatas and variation sets, and follow the standard classical forms.

Chopin, Frédéric (1810–1849, Poland)
Chopin wrote almost solely piano music, yet he is considered to be one of the greatest composers of the 19th century (and perhaps the greatest composer of piano music who has ever lived). Among his lyric masterpieces are preludes, waltzes, mazurkas, and nocturnes.

Debussy, Claude (1862–1918, France)
One of the most revolutionary composers for piano, Debussy represents the musical hallmark of French impressionism. Whole-tone and pentatonic scales, modes, and unusual tone colors produced through use of the pedals mark many of his works. His nontraditional approach to composition paved the way for many of the later 20th-century composers.

Diabelli, Anton (1781–1858, Austria)
Diabelli was best known in his day as the music publisher of Franz Schubert's works, as well as a composer of instructional music. His writing emulates the classical style, and his waltz tune inspired Beethoven's "Diabelli Variations."

Granados, Enrique (1867–1916, Spain)

Much of Granados' music is highly nationalistic, with lush harmonies, refined melodic lines, and stylistic rhythms. His piano music has been popularized by the brilliant pianist Alicia de Larrocha. Granados died when the cruise ship on which he was sailing as a passenger was torpedoed by a German submarine during World War I.

Grieg, Edvard (1843–1907, Norway)

Grieg's music is often associated with his Norwegian homeland, characterized by its pioneering spirit, rhythmic vitality, and lyricism. The influence of Robert Schumann can be felt in Grieg's music, dating from his early years as a student of Wenzel (Schumann's friend) at the Leipzig Conservatory. The ten books of *Lyric Pieces* are reminiscent of Schumann's short character pieces.

Heller, Stephen (1813–1888, Hungary)

Heller's studies and other short character pieces have been popular since their day. These works are exemplary preparation for the music of Chopin and Liszt, composers who were among Heller's friends. Exceptional melodic grace makes his etudes worthy of performance.

Kodály, Zoltán (1882–1967, Hungary)

Kodály is perhaps best known for his important contributions to music pedagogy, since he developed the curriculum and techniques of teaching for the Hungarian national music education system for children. His compositions reflect influences both from Hungarian folk music as well as impressionism.

MacDowell, Edward (1860–1908, USA)

MacDowell was America's first highly regarded serious composer. A very fine pianist himself, he was a brilliant miniaturist capable of composing playable, appealing character pieces as well as large-scale orchestral works such as his two piano concertos.

Marcello, Alessandro (1684–1750, Italy)

Alessandro Marcello did not depend on composition for a living. A versatile and well-rounded Venetian gentleman, he was known as a composer, poet, painter, philosopher, and mathematician. His oboe concertos were particularly highly regarded, catching the notice of J.S. Bach who transcribed his *Oboe Concerto in D minor* for keyboard (in this volume). Alessandro's younger brother, Benedetto, is sometimes incorrectly credited as composing this popular work.

Mendelssohn (-Bartholdy), Felix (1809–1847, Germany)

Mendelssohn's works are marked by a classical obsession with form, permeated with romantic lyricism and charm. He was highly regarded in his day as a composer, organist, pianist, conductor, and leader of musical society. His sister, Fanny Mendelssohn-Hensel, was also a fine composer. Mendelssohn penned 48 *Songs Without Words* as well as numerous other large- and small-scale works for piano.

Mozart, Wolfgang Amadeus (1756–1791, Austria)

Some consider Mozart to be the greatest musical genius who has ever lived. He gained international fame as a child prodigy performer and composer. His short life ended at age 35 after a sudden illness. Mozart's music is marked by a natural spontaneity of melodic line and a purity of musical form. His works are identified by K. (Köchel) numbers.

Muffat, Gottlieb (1690–1770, Germany)

Although Muffat spent most of his life in Vienna as court organist and music teacher, he was German by birth. His somewhat florid melodic treatment makes his music seem more French than German. His chief keyboard works were six suites and a chaconne, composed for Charles VI.

Pescetti, Giovanni Battista (1704–1766, Italy)

Pescetti was a Venetian organist and harpsichordist as well as a composer. He spent much of his professional life in London. At times, his music resembles that of Handel, a circumstance no doubt influenced by Handel's musical successes in that city.

Prokofiev, Sergei (1891–1953, Russia)

Prokofiev was acclaimed as a virtuoso pianist as well as a composer. Most of Prokofiev's piano music is very difficult; however, his piano works for children are accessible, balancing whimsy with biting irony.

Purcell, Henry (1659–1695, England)

Purcell is one of the most highly regarded of all English composers. Best known for his vocal compositions, his dramatic and expressive keyboard works include eight dance suites as well as numerous incidental pieces. His works are marked by their brevity as well as their charm.

Rachmaninoff, Sergei (1873–1943, Russia/USA)

Sergei Rachmaninoff, sometimes labeled "the melancholy Russian," is renowned for creating some of the most impassioned and sumptuous melodies ever written for piano. Although his dates place him in the 20th century, his compositional style is strongly romantic. He was a formidable virtuoso pianist, famed for his precision, rhythmic drive, languid tone, and awe-inspiring technical prowess.

Rimsky-Korsakov, Nikolay (1844–1908, Russia)

Rimsky-Korsakov was one of "The Russian Five," a group of five Russian composers who were proponents of native Russian music. Pianistically, Rimsky-Korsakov produced little which remains in the repertoire. He is best known for his richly orchestrated symphonic works.

Scarlatti, Domenico (1685–1757, Italy)

Scarlatti's more than 550 keyboard sonatas, originally written for harpsichord, often imitate the sound of the Spanish guitar and lute. His short sonatas, usually in rounded binary form, feature broad leaps and other virtuosic devices unusual for their time. His father was the eminent opera composer, Alessandro Scarlatti.

Wagner, Richard (1813–1883, Germany)

The fascinating life and career of Wagner encompassed two political exiles from his native Germany, the patronage of King Ludwig of Bavaria, a long-standing affair with the wife of one of his best friends, and a close personal relationship with Franz Liszt. Known almost entirely for his monumental-scale dramatic operas, Wagner's smaller works for piano have never been well known nor widely performed. However, they still exhibit his compositional trademarks–motivic treatment of melody, extreme harmonic chromaticism, and unabashed emotional content.

ALPHABETICAL LISTING OF CONTENTS BY TITLE